LET ME OUT!

LET ME OUT!
I'm a Prisoner in a Stained-Glass Jail

Wally Armbruster

MULTNOMAH · PRESS

Portland, Oregon 97266

Design by Wally Armbruster
Illustrated by Elizabeth Neilson Walker

LET ME OUT!
© 1985 by Multnomah Press
Portland, Oregon 97266

Printed in the United States of America

Armbruster, Wally.
    Let me out!

    1. Church renewal—Miscellanea. I. Title
BV600.2.A65   1985   269   85-11561
ISBN 0-88070-111-0

Publisher's Preface

It has now been several years since I first tentatively dipped into Wally Armbruster's **Bag of Noodles**. I felt uncomfortable. What manner of book would be printed to resemble a grocery sack? And what in the world did "noodles" have to do with Christian publishing?

My discomfort did not ease when I began reading. The artwork was . . . well, unconventional. The words were unconventional, too. They pricked, prodded, and sometimes annoyed me. So why did I keep reading? And why did those annoying thoughts stay with me so long after I'd put the book away? And why did it seem like the Lord was using the words of this Wally Armbruster (whoever he was) to penetrate neglected corners of my conscience?

Why was such an unconventional, uncomfortable book becoming one of my all-time favorites?

After reading the author's sequel, **Noodles Du Jour**, I could stand it no longer. On a cold, icy day in January I had one of our editors call him. Would there be any chance that Multnomah Press could publish some of this man's startling insights and penetrating wisdom?

The result of that conversation was **Let Me Out!**, the book you hold in your hands. I read the manuscript. It made me uncomfortable. How could we publish a book so pretentious, so non-traditional, so border-line irreverent?

Then the words began to work on me. I laughed. I winced, and I wept. There was really no question . . . we **had** to publish this book.

Please bear in mind, dear reader, that this was not meant to be a book of doctrine or theology. It is simply one man's opinion of what God might say if He stood behind the pulpit in your church next Sunday morning.

It may make you uncomfortable. It may annoy you. But there is a better than average chance that it will move you as no book has moved you in years.

"The problem of problems," wrote Wesley, "is to get Christianity into **life**." Wally Armbruster has done just that.

John Van Diest
Publisher
Multnomah Press

WHAT IF

GOD

HIMSELF

GAVE
NEXT
SUNDAY'S
SERMON?

(I WONDER WHAT
HE'D SAY?)

He
MIGHT
say:

LET ME OUT!

**I'm a prisoner in
a stained-glass
jail!**

Why

. . . my Roman Catholics, Episcopalians, Presbyterians, Lutherans, Methodists, Baptists, Fundamentalists, and others who are the Christian church . . .

Why

do you confine me so?

Why

have you become so content to limit the scope of The Church to what goes on inside of the church-house walls?

Why do you think it's enough
to embalm Me in a Gothic tomb,
surrounded by somber and severe symbols
   where you come to sit like rigid robots
      in perpendicular pews,
         holding heavy hymnals
            in medieval museums or modern mausoleums?

I've often wondered:

Why do you honor Me
with ritual that bores you?

When did I say that I demand
                                    (or even like)
       rote and repetitious ritual?

       When did I express a special fondness for

              16th century liturgy
              17th century calligraphy
              18th century songs
       or
              19th century revival meetings?

When did I tell you that gathering together to worship on Sunday

must seem like a dutiful chore . . .

to be carried on forevermore in the tradition of

your ancestors . . .

and devoid of expression
   of **your**
         own
            generation?

I DON'T REMEMBER.

In fact, I don't remember
ever saying that
the **essence**
of
My church is ecclesiastical

        . . . or liturgical

        . . . or ceremonial

        . . . or institutional.

BUT I DO PRIZE YOUR PRAISE AND THANKSGIVING

and
I will accept it in whatever
style or language helps
you express it
best.

Yet even if you

**Clap your hands and
raise your voices . . .**

Even if you **FILL** the church-house
for every service . . .
it isn't enough.

**I ask more of the Church
than praise and thanksgiving.**

I am not a rare champagne to be kept on a shelf in a velvet closet, cere- moniously brought out to be sipped only on a feast day.

I AM YOUR DAILY BREAD

I WANT TO **LIVE** WITH YOU

LET ME OUT

of
the
church-house
and into your apartments.
       your houses,
       condominiums,
       and flats.

I want to be with you in the bathroom

when you brush your teeth

or take a shower.

I belong in the kitchen
and the bedroom
and the family room
when you're watching TV.

I want to be in your supermarkets
and shopping centers,
your office buildings
and factories . . .

to ride in your Cadillacs and Chevettes,
your DC-9s and your space shuttles.

**I am not just for Sundays
or for grace-before-meals.**

I WANT TO BE POPULAR

   . . . like Robert Redford, baseball,
      McDonald's hamburgers, Levi's,
      and Coca-Cola.

I want to be on your lips in public

   . . . naturally . . . like those songs you sing along
with in your stereos and transistors . . . like
politics and sports and the weather.

Of course, some of My people already **DO** this —
especially those who identify themselves as "born-again
Christians"

— whom some of you, derisively, call "Jesus freaks" or "fanatics."

Why do these people embarrass you,
My institutional   church people?

Why does it embarrass you to hear a God fanatic say out loud in public:

"PRAISE THE LORD" or "JESUS SAVES"

Yet it doesn't embarrass you at all to hear fanatics of another kind shout:

"HOORAY FOR THE DALLAS COWBOYS!" or "DEEEEEE - FENSE!"
in a jammed Superdome???

If God Himself gave next Sunday's sermon, I wonder if He might say:

I TOLD YOU NOT TO TAKE MY NAME IN VAIN.

Now you seldom take my name at all.

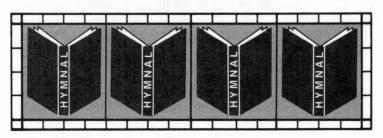

except in the safe sanctuary of a rote prayer
or a church-house hymn.

AN APOSTOLIC CHURCH CANNOT MERELY TOLL BELLS TO CALL PEOPLE TO GOD . . .

. . . nor wait for converts to come
for Bible class or instruction.

It must go OUT to where the people are.

A LOT OF THEM
ARE SITTING
IN FRONT OF A
TELEVISION SET

The electronic church may not be all it ought to be. But they are doing **some** job, for sure, and seven days a week.

And there are **millions** of them . . .
    not only **watching,**
        but also preaching the Word,
            giving **witness,**
                and doing **missionary work.**

In fact,

    though there is a lot on the screens of your movie
    houses, TV sets, and VCRs that is working **against**
    Me

My Message has sometimes been preached
more effectively
on Walton's Mountain
and in
The Little House on the Prairie
than from
the pulpits of My church-houses.

PLEASE DON'T GET ANGRY OR MISUNDERSTAND WHAT I'M SAYING.

I LOVE THE CHURCH

I challenge you so because you are **needed** so.

The church is:

Needed by Me . . . because I **chose** to
spread My Word **through you.**

Needed by so many outside the church:
Those who are lost and searching for Me
Those who are bewildered and confused
Those who are empty
Those millions who are hanging on by
their fingernails
Those who have despaired

And the **church** needs the church —
its outward signs
its strength in numbers
its ordained ministers and priests
its schools and its church-houses

. . . just as they need the Bible and prayer and even a
place to tithe.

But where has the VITALITY gone ??

Has your concern for "separation of church and state"
caused separation of **Me** from your daily life?

IN RENDERING TO CAESAR,

HAVE YOU
RENDERED <u>ME?</u>

I am not running for election as "America's official God."
Nor **any** other nation's God.

Yet all over the world,
nations and divisions of nations are shedding blood
and venting hate
armied as Moslems or Christians or Jews —
as if I am **sponsoring** them
in some kind of sick war
of God vs. Allah vs. Yahweh vs. Jesus Christ.

And even Christians are fighting Christians — not
only in the streets of Ireland but also in the political
arenas everywhere.

I am being **used.**
My name is being taken in vain.

I am not so concerned
about whether American children
are allowed to utter prayers
in public schools
as whether they (or **adults**)
REALLY PRAY at all.

**What counts is whether
you <u>mean it</u> or not.**

Take, for example: America's **Money**.

Curiously, though I have been banned from the classroom,
My Name is still on your currency and coin.

It says:

"IN GOD WE TRUST"

I sometimes smile at that.
IS IT A JOKE?
Some of the things you spend that money for
— well it ought to make you wonder:

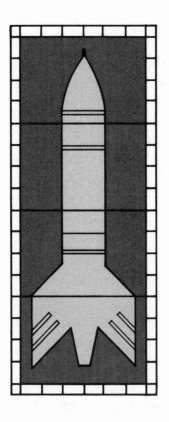

Does the billions of it
you spend on
bombs and missiles
indicate that you put
more of your trust
in your arsenals
than you do in Me?

<u>Even as individuals</u> . . .

YOU SEEM TO TRUST PRUDENTIAL
MORE THAN PROVIDENCE . . .

an iron-clad contract
more than My covenant . . .

a handgun
more than a prayer.

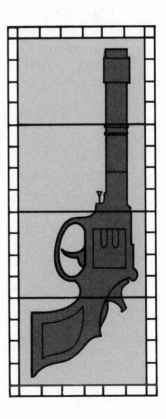

In God you trust?

Then:

WHY DO YOU DEPEND MORE FOR YOUR FEELING OF SECURITY ON BOOZE OR BARBITURATES OR ON BANK ACCOUNTS OR BAUBLES . . . OR ON REPRISALS YOU CAN USE TO BRANDISH BEFORE THOSE WHO POSE A THREAT TO YOUR AUTHORITY OR POCKETBOOK, YOUR PETROLEUM **OR** YOUR PRIDE.

And when Caesar

    — in the form of corporation or government
    or social pressure —

does something that you KNOW I would
  not approve of . . .

    WHY
     IS
      THE
       CHURCH
      SO

           silent

          ?

THE CHURCH SHOULD BE **AS** CONCERNED WITH

RIGHT and **RIGHTS**
AS IT IS WITH
RITES.

Is challenging Caesar only for
the Christian weirdos and crazies
— the handful of 20th-century-fools-for-Christ
who are willing to risk their lives
(or reputations)
for causes they identify as
My causes?

Is that why they must still
"go it alone"
or as upstart ecumenical groups . . .
BECAUSE NO OFFICIAL CHURCH BODY
WOULD STICK ITS NECK OUT?

   . . . as happened at Selma? At Washington, D.C.?

                              and at Calvary?

WHERE ARE YOU . . .
(my powerful,
organized church)

> when they picket or sit-in,
> bumper-sticker or challenge
> or demonstrate in My Name?

WHY,
My established church and hierarchy, do
you blush, hide, tut-tut,
and deny them even consideration
of your support
when they want to
"disturb the peace"
or
"challenge the law"?

God knows
    (and Christ
        certainly demonstrated)

THE PEACE
SOMETIMES
NEEDS TO BE
DISTURBED

AND
MAN'S
LAWS
OR
CUSTOMS
NEED
TO BE
CHALLENGED.

Peace is not
"staying out of it"
or
"keeping your nose clean."

Peace is not
"minding your own business."

PEACE IS MINDING
MY BUSINESS

It is the only Peace there is.
And that makes it a **mission**
for the **church** —
a requirement that the church
get involved
by disturbing
whatever disturbs
My peace.

If other "power groups"
and "special interests"
have lobbyists,
shouldn't the church?

If other interests can get hearings in state houses and world
courts . . . and even in corporate board rooms . . . why
shouldn't the church? Should your voice not be heard?

The **missionary** work of the church
should not be confined to faraway places
among primitive tribes.

It needs to be done, too,
right where you live
in so-called
"civilized" society.

As in all missionary work,
it involves **risk.**

BUT DO YOU NOT KNOW
THAT I WILL BE THERE
WITH YOU?

That is the point of My cry to
LET ME OUT OF THE STAINED-GLASS JAIL.

Because, you see, if you don't confine ME you will stop
confining YOURSELVES (My church) to the routine of
pomp and ceremony, of bringing Me gold and
frankincense and myrrh.

Bring Me instead
your witness, your commitment,
your activism.

41

It's not enough to "make Me your God"
  — to be My church —
    only when you play hymns on electric organs
    or electric guitars.

            I want to be your God
            and you to be My church
            when you play commerce
            and industry on
                electronic word processors
                and computers

                        . . . and
              when you play politics
                in City Hall and
                the United Nations.

It's not enough to worship Me and adore Me
as some kind of historical figure like George Washington.

I want to be worn on your sleeve
— like the alligator on your Izod shirt.

Take Me out of your pocket
and pin Me on your lapel
as you do with your lodge emblem,
your country's flag,
or your company's logo.

Display Me openly
— and at least as proudly —
as you do the Rolex on your wrist
or the diamond ring on your finger.

WHAT THE CHURCH NEEDS NOW

is

SAINTS NOW,

MARTYRS NOW,

and

MIRACLES NOW

It's up to you to provide the saints and martyrs.
I will provide the miracles.

Why do you preach and talk about
  sainthood,
    martyrdom,
      and
        miracles
        only in the past tense???

They did not stop
on the last page of the Bible.

Have my miracles of
  spring,
    water,
      birth,
        mother-love
          . . . and brussels sprouts . . .
ceased to be miracles because you take
them for granted???

You'd be surprised how many miracles I do **every day.**

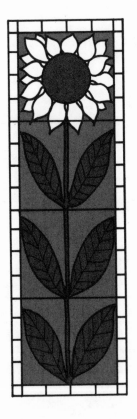

For people who **believe,** I still do as many as **ever.**

And saints?
They surround you!

But you seldom see them
and are reluctant
to proclaim them.

And that makes it difficult
for them to proclaim themselves
as saints.

By continuing to recognize only biblical saints
or canonized saints,
you make it seem that the church
has no
saints-of-the-moment.

You make it seem indecent
or egotistical
or sacrilegious
for a
Tom or Dick or Harry
or a
Jane, Jill, or Mary
to say:
"Yes, I'm a saint"
as easily as they say,
"Yes, I'm a lawyer"
or
"Yes, I'm a Lutheran."

IT DOESN'T TAKE A SUPERSTAR TO BE A SAINT.
IF YOU CONFESS CHRIST, YOU ARE A SAINT.

I don't demand perfection . . .
only that you **strive** for perfection.

I don't demand achievement . . .
only that you **try** to achieve.

IF ONLY YOU WOULD
USE
THE TALENTS I GAVE YOU!!!

. . . BUT I expect you to use that talent
for your **sainthood** . . .
not merely for your **livelihood.**

And I expect the CHURCH —as a body— to
marshal the talents of all its individual members
into the awesome strength of its one, holy,
catholic and apostolic
potential.

Yes .... awesome!!!

But so far, it is an unrealized potential:

un<u>realiz</u>ed . . . and therefore unrealized.

The church
must be more than

    a. CLERGY (to conduct the services)

              and

    b. LAITY (to attend the services and put something in
        the collection basket)

                    The church must be

                    a 7-DAY CHURCH

            . . . not just a "Sunday" church.

Today,
My church
needs more clearly-identified **worker**-saints:

CARPENTERS and FOOD PROCESSORS

SENATORS and SECRETARIES

LAWYERS and CAPTAINS OF INDUSTRY

MOVIEMAKERS and HOMEMAKERS

DOCKWORKERS and DISC JOCKEYS

PASTORS and PREACHERS

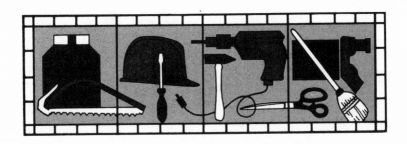

In the olden days,
My church
clearly had **worker**-saints:

CARPENTERS and FISHERMEN

TAX-COLLECTORS and TOGA MAKERS

SHEPHERDS and SHIP CAPTAINS

WEAVERS and HOMEMAKERS

POETS and PHARISEES

PASTORS and PREACHERS

If you all get together as a church of 7-day saints . . .

. . . can you imagine the effect on the world when the
saints really **do** come marching in?

For example . . .

Consider the potential
of
"Apostles in Pin-Stripe Suits"!

**You, the part of My church
who are in**

MARKETING and ADVERTISING:

HOW IS IT THAT YOU CAN BE SO
SUCCESSFUL AT MARKETING such things as

. . . detergents and dog food
. . . air conditioners and hair conditioners
. . . instant coffee and disposable diapers
. . . junk food and jogging shoes
. . . plastic plants and Barbie dolls
. . . beer and soft drinks and cigarettes and
  every conceivable kind of labor-saving
  device from electric can-openers to garage-
  door openers . . .

BUT YOU CANNOT MARKET ME?

Why can't My church get these
marketing experts together
and come up with a **marketing plan**
to market Me?

I may not be a push-button God
but
nothing you sell is more responsive.

I may not come in a disposable container,
but you could make a point of the fact
that I don't louse up the environment.

I last longer than
Forever batteries
or
Midas mufflers.

I stress the point,
My marketing-expert apostles:

MY SHARE-OF-MARKET IS DECLINING.

And it's your job to reverse the trend.

It isn't enough to put a share of your money
in the Sunday collection.

I want a share of your **expertise**
. . . and the talent I gave you.

And you **ADVERTISING** geniuses:

How is it that you can write and produce such
creative commercials for parity products or a
Xerox copier
   . . . but you can't do as well for The Original?

Now there's a creative challenge for you:
sell Me to the masses.
   And I don't mean just on Sunday morning TV
   or on CBN.

I want prime time.

Could you do it?

I think you'd find Me an ideal client to work for. You
could run anything you think is good. No need to bring
Me copy or storyboards for approval
    . . . just let your conscience be your guide.

            I'd leave it up to you
            whether to use jingles, slice-of-life, animation,
            or testimonials. I am not fond of hard-sell
            — but that doesn't rule out some pretty tough
            straight-talk. Maybe it's even time for some
            scare tactics.

            You've never shied from using adjectives like
            "heavenly" or **"out-of-this-world"**
            to describe fabric-softeners or cream rinse
            or cake mix . . .

            so, in advertising **Me,** you can go as far
            as you like. I can live up to any superlative
            or claim you care to make.

This job opportunity
applies not only to advertising people
but also to

SALESMEN OF ALL KINDS.

If you're as good a salesman
or saleswoman as you think you are,
we need you.

You're out there pounding the pavement,
making the calls.

How good are you at selling **ME?**
HAVE YOU HONESTLY EVER TRIED?

The first twelve members of
The Christian Sales Force
were not particularly articulate
(until Pentecost anyway)
and they had no experience,
          no sales-aids,
          no expense account.

BUT THEY WERE MIGHTILY EFFECTIVE.
They **believed** in what they were selling.

And the few of you
whom I've blessed with a talent for

SPEECHMAKING:

. . . the ones so often
asked to "make the
presentation" for your
company or to give
luncheon or after-dinner
speeches before
professional or civic or
social organizations:

DO YOU WORK ME INTO YOUR TALK SOMEHOW?

**It's easy.
And I expect it, you know.**

**In fact,
why aren't you** the ones in the pulpit
instead of those who
— though good pastors and ministers —
give dull sermons?

With My Word and your talent,
we could fill the pews again.

You **LAWYERS:**

In your cases or counsel,
do you represent **Me . . .**
as well as you represent your clients?

I expect it.

Does it disturb you that half the world seems to
be suing the other half . . .
through every available loophole, for every conceivable cent?

That may be good for your business but it's bad
for Mine.
It breeds hate, animosity, revenge, reciprocity.

> You have marvelous opportunity to sow
> the seeds of peace instead of
> confrontation.

And you know what the Bible says about peacemakers.

And if you worry that it would
cut into your fees, don't.

I will stake my reputation as a Judge on this:
You will be handsomely rewarded.

You, My **TOP-MANAGEMENT EXECUTIVES:**

How is it that you are so effective and dynamic
as shepherds of your companies and
corporations, yet so many of you are content to
be **sheep** as members of your church?

If the church is "losing business" who
better than **you** to lead it in the other
direction?

If you are a pillar of the business
community or industrial community,
why are you not also
a pillar of the church?

I GAVE YOU YOUR TALENT FOR LEADERSHIP.

I expect you to use it for My Business as well
as for yours.

That's why, in the operation of your company's business, I
caution you not to think of yourselves as Big Shots but as
laborers in My vineyard.

Regard yourselves not so much as owners
but as **stewards**
— because I will hold you accountable.

Your stockholders may judge your performance by the
bottom line. **I** will judge your performance by **how you
get to** the bottom line:

> by the way you treat your employees, your
> customers, and your suppliers. And yes, even
> your competitors.

It may sound difficult. But it's easier than you think. It **is**
possible to please us both.

But there can be no question about Which of us
is First Priority.

I've heard it said that, for Corporate Executives,
"It's lonely at the top."

It's lonely only
if you lock Me out of your private office
and your Board Room.

You would be surprised how **much**
I would help
if you would ask Me
into your executive life.

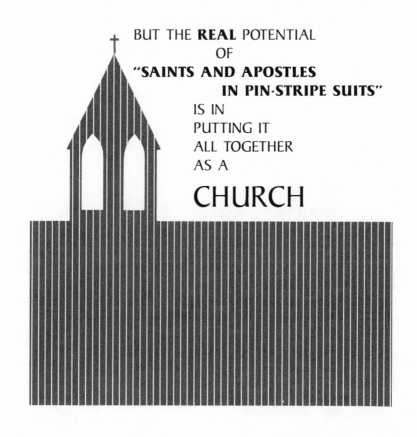

BUT THE **REAL** POTENTIAL
OF
**"SAINTS AND APOSTLES
IN PIN-STRIPE SUITS"**
IS IN
PUTTING IT
ALL TOGETHER
AS A

CHURCH

CONSIDER THIS:

**If you can come together at the
church-house
to pray . . .
why can't you also come together there
to pool your resources and expertise?**

For example:
When the advertising man heard My challenge he
said, "Hold on, God! Yes, I could and would write
ads and commercials about you — but who
would pay to put them on prime-time TV or in
the newspaper?"

What would you answer him?

My answer was this:

HOW IS IT THAT A **GROUP OF PEOPLE**
CALLED A **COMPANY** OR **CORPORATION**
    OR **CLUB** OR **ASSOCIATION**
CAN ROUTINELY DO WHAT A GROUP OF FOLKS
CALLED A
CHURCH
CONSIDERS IMPOSSIBLE?

As a church —
    with executive, marketing, selling, advertising,
    administrative, secretarial, managerial, financial, legal,
    technical, and mechanical specialists of every kind and
    description

YOU WILL FIND WAYS TO DO
MOST **ANYTHING**
YOU DETERMINE TO DO.

It would take RISK and SACRIFICE.

But how is it that you can risk and sacrifice
so much to win
a **new client** or **court case**
   or **election** or **sales contest**
or to launch a new product
or enter a new market . . .

   yet you can't (or won't) apply the same
   talents, risk, and sacrifice
   to winning recognition
   for the One
   who gave you all those talents in the first place?

IS THIS ASKING TOO MUCH?

That's for **you** to decide, not Me.

But I assure you: it's the most important decision you will ever be asked to make.

You see, it isn't just "the fruits of your labor" that I want.

Nor is it the labor itself · though that is infinitely closer. What I want is **YOU.**

(And there are no asterisks.)

And . . . if God Himself gave next Sunday's
sermon . . . He MIGHT go on to say:

THERE IS HOMILY HERE
FOR EACH
OF YOU
IN EVERY WALK OF LIFE
AND EVERY VOCATION . . .
YOUR CALLING
MUST BE BLENDED WITH
MY CALLING

For ARCHITECTS

Think what you could do!

- a place to pray in a private home?

- a chapel in a shopping mall or office building or park or condominium or airport?

- a poustinia for somebody's place-in-the-country?

And the church-house itself:

Why only the big hall for all, with pews?
Why not also a small place for small
groups? Why not a tiny place for someone
to meditate alone . . . perhaps with a way
for him or her to choose music to suit that
person's own vibes or mood?

Why not a garden . . . not merely
to look at but to **be** in. For
some, "nearer to God in
a garden" is true.
Could everything else
look . . . uh . . . well, less
severe: softer . . .
homier?

Just for the record:
I am not all that fond of GOLD.
Or silver.
I realize that the world values it
because there's so little of it.

You could also reason that
I made so little of it because
it wasn't one of My favorite creations.

You'll notice that the things
I like the most
are the things I made a **lot** of:
Trees.
Sky.
Wildflowers.
Water.

You architects might keep that in mind.

(And incidentally —

I have nothing against stained-glass windows.
That isn't the point I am trying to make to
My church.)

YOU SERVICE PEOPLE:

shopkeepers and schoolteachers
doctors and nurses
waiters and housekeepers
policemen and firemen
government/public utilities workers
cabdrivers and bank tellers
. . . and all others
who meet the public . . .

HAVE YOU NOTICED THAT
SOME OF YOU ARE MISERABLE
AND
SOME OF YOU ARE HAPPY
                    . . . IN THE SAME JOB?

It has little to do with whether you
"attend church" or not.

THE ONES WHO HATE THE JOB
NEVER TAKE ME TO WORK WITH THEM.

> The job is drudgery-for-a-paycheck.
> The boss is an overpaid ogre.
> The people they serve and the tasks they do are
>   ditches to be dug and obstacles to overcome on
>   the way to five o'clock.
> It's hell on earth.

THE ONES WHO ARE HAPPY
TAKE ME TO WORK WITH THEM.

> They see the people (even the boss) as brothers and
> sisters . . . as fellow-children of God . . . maybe
> cranky and selfish at times, but nevertheless potential
> co-heirs to heaven.

> Even in doing the tasks and the paperwork, they see
> the people they serve behind the tasks and the
> paperwork.

> It may not be heaven on earth.
> But it is what heaven is all about.

Try it. Take me to work with you.
See ME in the people you serve.

> The nastiest job on earth can be . . . glorious!

YOU PEOPLE IN THE ARTS

. . . painters and photographers
film-makers and writers
comic-strip and puzzle-makers
TV producers and musicians
singers and actors
potters and sculptors
athletes and comedians . . .

In the early days, it was the church
who supported you.

Now it is time for you to support
the church. Yet many of you do not even recognize
yourself as the church . . .
nor recognize Me.

EVEN THOSE WHO HAVE BECOME

"STARS"
ARE STARS-WITHOUT-A-HEAVEN

They have achieved "fame and fortune" beyond their
wildest dreams . . .
  yet have not found what they're looking for.

THEY ARE LOOKING FOR **ME.**

So many are lost, cynical, unhappy, selfish
  . . . perhaps suicidal.
They seek solace in drugs, alcohol, sex, sports cars
  . . . but solace never comes.

      ESPECIALLY for artistic people
       . . . being estranged from Me can tear you apart.

                    Do you know why?

Because your GIFT
is a special part of ME.

I am ART.

When artistic people find Me

— as many do —

it is for them a HIGH
beyond belief . . . the ultimate in the "born-again"
experience.

But sadly, even artists who profess some measure
of faith in God
actually use My gift
against Me.

Why do you use the power of your talent to make sin attractive?

BECAUSE IT SELLS?

Or is it because you can't think of anything else?

WHAT **GREAT** THINGS YOU COULD DO
WITH YOUR TALENT . . . **FOR** ME!

I am not talking about "holy pictures" in the traditional sense of that term.

But if you can be so prolific and arouse such frenzy and passion using such subjects as
sex, crime, divorce, scandal, violence, politics, and competitive sports . . .

YOU WOULD BE **AMAZED**
BY WHAT YOU COULD DO
WITH **LOVE**
AS YOUR SUBJECT.

I'm not talking about "moon-June-spoon" romantic love or "hugging-people" or even new expressions of Bible stories.

I'm talking about using Me as the SOURCE of your art.

I am Love.
And I am completely contemporary.

If you plug Me
into your easels and typewriters,
　　　your Magic Markers and your cameras,
　　　your guitars and your amplifiers,
　　　your baseball bats and tennis rackets,
　　　your potters' wheels and spinning wheels,
　　　your microphones and your funny bones . . .

YOU WILL NEVER RUN OUT OF MATERIAL!!!

I will remind you (in case you have forgotten)
that I invented everything you use:

HUMOR	MUSIC	ANGER
BEAUTY	BIRTH	LAWS
TEARS	DEATH	RIGHT FROM
AFFECTION	SELFLESSNESS	WRONG
PLAY	MOTHERHOOD	PARTING
WORK	FATHERHOOD	REUNION
PEACE	CHILDHOOD	DISCOVERY
EGO	ADOLESCENCE	RISK
NEED FOR LOVE	SURPRISE	STRUGGLE
NEED TO LOVE	TOGETHERNESS	FAITHFULNESS
TENDERNESS	TOUGHNESS	TOUCHING
RESPONSIBILITY	FEAR	INTELLIGENCE
FREEDOM	EXHILARATION	LAUGHTER
COLOR	PASSION	FEELING

. . .and, oh yes: in case you are under the
impression that the devil did it, I was the One
who invented SEX.

The most artistic thing I ever did was create FREE WILL.

As an artist, you may use . . . or **misuse** . . . the talent I gave you.

If you are truly talented, you will use My wellspring . . . and not the devil's or the world's . . . and your work will **sell.**

PEOPLE ARE STARVING FOR IT!

To artists of all kinds I say:

Volunteer.

You could revitalize the church-house and the Sunday school. You could bring joy to My house. You could make Me **alive** . . . Me **felt** . . . make Me **exciting.**

Excitement needs to be put into Christianity.
It needs it . . .

                         . . . in the **best** way.

Remember:

whenever you call on your artistic juices
. . . whenever you need inspiration . . .
you would do well to call on Me for help.

I COULD FEED YOU SOME IDEAS.

In case you haven't noticed:
I've done some pretty artistic things Myself.

And you, the members of My church who
WORK WITH THE SKILL OF YOUR HANDS,
the **BLESSING OF YOUR BRAWN,**
and by the **SWEAT OF YOUR BROW . . .**

My carpenters, plumbers, electricians,
bricklayers, truck drivers, house painters,
tile-setters, mechanics, machinists,
assembly-line workers, housekeepers and
hairdressers, ditch-diggers and farmworkers . . .

**YOU, TOO, SHOULD GIVE ME SOME
"DIRECT LABOR."**

In earlier times, the church-house was built and maintained by its own people, using the skills of their trades.

THAT WAS "OFFERTORY" AT ITS BEST.

Why couldn't you do it again?
Believe Me, the whole feeling of **being** the church would be magnified.

Doing something for your God is a much more precious gift than "helping to pay to have it done."

You can also use your "trade" to give witness in other ways:
You, too, can TAKE ME TO WORK WITH YOU.

You can help shatter the myth among "macho" men that
God is only for women and children.

You can tell them for Me that My saints
— some frail —
are the strongest people on earth.

And if they think that
My angels are all cherubs
. . . in pink tutus with gossamer wings . . .
wait 'til they shake hands with Michael!

You can also give witness by giving a day's work for a day's pay.

It isn't only your employer who expects it.
I expect it, too.

To give less is stealing.

And
if it makes you feel any better,
I have the same rules
for your employer:
   a day's pay for a day's work.

You see, rendering to Caesar
and rendering to God
are not
mutually exclusive.

And don't overlook this:

USE YOUR SKILL AND SWEAT (ALONE OR WITH OTHERS) IN VOLUNTEER WORK. THE POOR ALWAYS NEED SOMETHING TO BE FIXED OR BUILT. YOU, IN MY NAME, CAN PERFORM AN ABUNDANCE OF MIRACLES!!!

Miracles?

Perhaps your fixing of a poverty-stricken widow's toilet or insulating a welfare family's freezing flat — for free — is not your standard idea of what constitutes a miracle.

But I assure you: it's Mine.

Doing things for others — through you — is one of the best miracles I do.

You, the **REST OF THE CHURCH . . .**

> (those I haven't mentioned specifically by
> occupation or talent)

. . . you can certainly find your message in there
somewhere. This is, after all, not a "parts list" or spec
sheet on
"How to Build and Maintain the Church."

It's more exactly a Love Letter
from your Father and Brother.

If I find fault, it's only because
I know your enormous unrealized potential.
Though I made you mortal,
I also made you immortal.

Being creatures of habit,
you have some habits to get **out of.**
And some to get **into.**

I concentrate here on your habit of
making "church"
almost entirely a Sunday-worship thing.
The other side of the same coin
is your habit
of pursuing earthly goals
without realizing that
that **pursuit**
is **part** of your pursuit of heavenly goals.

Make Me your habit.

In closing,
I have a special message
for My
special church people:

the CLERGY

I love you.
   You love Me.
      You love the church.
         You try.
            You do everything the church asks.
               You try to adapt to changing times without
                  compromising My basic principles . . . or your
                  own.

BUT . . .

You're discouraged.
You lament:

            "Why isn't anything happening?"
         "Nobody cares. Nobody listens anymore."
         "The old stand-bys still come . . . but passively,
            phlegmatically, like sheep."
            "But where are their lambs?"

And the seminaries are even emptier than the pews.

For starters,
you could stop polishing the silver so much.

In many cases, you are featuring the candlestick
more than you feature the Light.

They will not be attracted by the dogma, the
theology, the liturgy, the sermons, the hymns,
or even the Bible.

They will not come until they see the Light.

I am the Light.

The church's rituals and its institutions
are the wiring and the fixtures.
I am the Electricity.

**Are you selling the church too much
and Me too little?**

IT IS TIME FOR RENAISSANCE.

I will not tell you how.
I will tell you only that you **can.**

But I will give you
a few things to consider.

For one thing
you should be let out of
the stained-glass jail . . .
freed from being so church-house
only oriented.

I'm not suggesting that
the church-house be
destroyed, abandoned,
or even lessened in
importance—merely
that the horizons be
broadened.

I'm not advocating
either conservatism
or liberalism. In fact,
at times, the liberals
so staunchly conserve
their liberalism that
it's hard to discern
the difference.

Structured non-structure seems strikingly the same as
structured structure.

HAVE YOU CONSIDERED THAT THERE IS VIRTUE IN THEM ALL?

Structure and Non-structure
  Tradition and Novelty
    Experience and Experiment
     Congregation and Cloister
      Formality and Informality

    A time to sing
     A time to shout
      A time to clap your hands
       but also a time to keep quiet
       and just listen to me.

OPEN YOUR WINDOWS

including the windows of your mind and soul

**There still is but One Shepherd
. . . but more flocks and fragments
of flocks than ever.**

The world's obsession **with winning**
. . . in games, in business, in politics, in schools,
in society, and even in marriage and family . . .
has not escaped the church.

Some of you have been so intent on winning an
honest disagreement over some doctrinal or
procedural point that you have splintered My church.

Be sure you LISTEN
. . . with **love** . . .
to viewpoints and interpretations
different from your own.

IF YOU DIFFER . . .

**before you build it into another issue that
isolates or divorces or estranges one Christian
body from another**

BE SURE THAT YOUR POINT OF DIFFERENCE
IS SOMETHING THAT WOULD
MAKE A DIFFERENCE TO **ME!**

OPEN YOUR
WINDOWS, TOO,
TO A BROADENED VIEW
OF WHAT IT
TAKES TO BE
A CLERGYMAN.

Must he or she
be a Xerox copy
of what the
church has come
to regard as the
"type": well-groomed,
soft-spoken,
gentlemanly,
formal, scholarly
(perhaps even a
little dull)?

Could not a minister
have just
1 talent?

(You might re-read the
first letter of Paul to
the Corinthians.)

Could an ordained minister be a specialist?

SALESMAN . . . someone who couldn't pass math or Greek but who could sell ice to Eskimos . . . and chooses to sell God to man.

PREACHER . . . someone especially good at turning on groups of people. The best of these could appear on radio, TV, or videocassettes.

PASTOR . . . someone who may be pathetic in the pulpit . . . and thin on theology . . . but super as a shepherd: understanding and loving, wise and just.

THEOLOGIAN & SCHOLAR . . . who may not be very good at dealing with people but terrific at thinking and at giving insightful interpretation and understanding of My Word.

TEACHER . . . who has a special talent for explaining things (even theology) in "plain folks" terms.

WRITER . . . who can teach on paper (and make it exciting).

LITURGIST . . . who can create stimulating forms of congregational church experience within the bounds of orthodoxy but without the bonds of tradition.

SOCIAL WORKER . . . blessed with the patience and compassion to minister to people with special problems — in hospitals, prisons, ghettos, universities, bus stations, etc.

MUSICIAN, SINGER, PAINTER, SCULPTOR, PHOTOGRAPHER, OR POET . . . to capture My Word and Spirit and inspire My Love in their unique "language" and special pulpits.

CONFESSOR . . . who can specialize in listening, consoling, and healing — one sinner at a time.

EXECUTIVE, ADMINISTRATOR, MARKETING DIRECTOR . . . who can specialize in running a church's "business."

POLITICIAN . . . who can be the church's lobbyist.

BUSINESS/INDUSTRY CHAPLAIN . . . who can manage to get elected to the Board of Directors of corporations or unions, to represent ethics and morality; or to be available to employees or executives with problems. Is that far-fetched? Listen, you can make a case for it:

Companies spend tons of money sending employees to psychiatrists, alcohol or drug centers, or hospitals — for conditions that exist primarily because they are estranged from Me. My believers are the best, most dependable employers and employees on earth. And you can document that if you put your mind to it.

MONASTICS . . . who could serve Me in a special way. Perhaps just for a year or so, not necessarily for life. There could be a monastic clergy but also a monastic laity.

MISSIONARIES . . . people who are willing and eager to go anywhere to spread My Word: whether to strange or hostile countries or to strange and hostile neighborhoods.

ENTREPRENEURS . . . those who think of **new** ministries or new missions outside the established ones — and who are adventurous enough to want to DO them.

That's enough to give you the idea.

A vibrant and vital clergy
will cause bulging seminaries
and do wonders toward
causing a vibrant and vital church.

For certain,
you cannot continue to cling to the notion
that a seventeenth-century clergy
can serve a twentieth-century church.

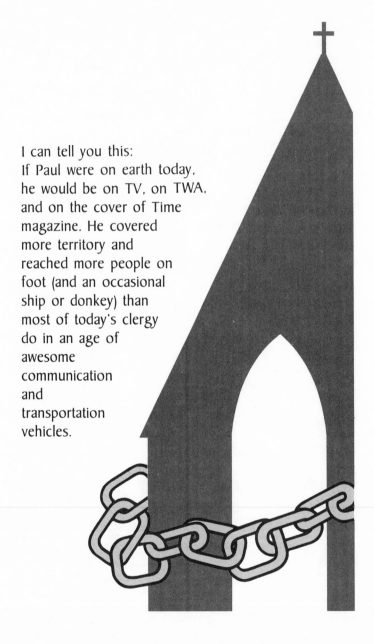

I can tell you this:
If Paul were on earth today,
he would be on TV, on TWA,
and on the cover of Time
magazine. He covered
more territory and
reached more people on
foot (and an occasional
ship or donkey) than
most of today's clergy
do in an age of
awesome
communication
and
transportation
vehicles.

UNCHAIN YOURSELVES
FROM THE CHURCH-HOUSE.

Be **less** concerned with methodology, theology,
ecclesiology — and whatever else separates you into sects
and synods.

Be more concerned . . .
in fact, be **consumed** . . .

with

THE MESSAGE:

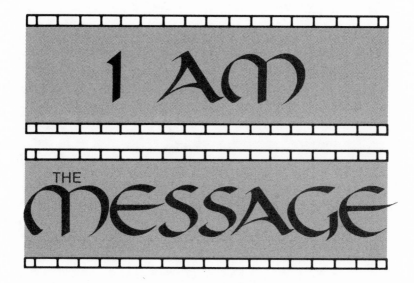

Deliver It . . .

. . . EVERYWHERE.

Amen.

An Afterword

from the author
(who doesn't like Forewords)

When I was a child, I thought of "the church" only as a **place:** the big building with a steeple and stained-glass windows.

Later, I came to regard "the church" also as the ecclesiastical officialdom - the clergy and especially the hierarchy who dealt with theological matters and decided what we would "do" in "church."

Finally, during the sixties, I heard someone say, "The church is YOU!"

I remember thinking, **"Who, ME?"**

Eventually I got used to the idea. And rather liked it. I understood (I thought) both the meaning and implications of "the church" as **all of its people** . . . and of lay-ministry for **every** Christian.

Then, in the seventies, I wrote a few Christian books - rather off-the-wall, cartoony things which I have called "sneaky Jesus books" because they look more "earthy" than heavenly. I received a lot of letters and telephone calls from **non**-mainline-church Christian people, was invited to speak at various Christian conventions and seminars, appeared as a guest on the PTL television show . . . and in other ways was exposed to (for me) a whole new spectrum of Christians I had previously only heard about or read about.

Until then, most of the people I knew were mainline-church Christians: primarily Roman Catholics, Lutherans, Methodists, or Episcopalians. If asked, we'd identify ouselves according to denomination or generally as Christians. But that's about as far as it ever went.

I mean - we didn't really TALK about . . .

"JESUS"

. . . out loud like that . . . except in church. In fact, we did not really talk about church, except in the sense of "I'll see you in church" or "On the way to church Sunday . . ."

Even most of the priests and ministers I knew (with a few notable exceptions) were pretty "cool" about Jesus - other than the "historical" Jesus. They were far more vocal about theological or liturgical issues than the core issue that Jesus Christ is Savior and lives NOW . . . or that the Holy Spirit is with us, whether we're in a downtown elevator or making out our income tax report.

Most of us have been far more interested in persuading people to belong to the church or to **attend** church than to BE the church.

But those "other Christians" I've met in recent years are somethin' else. Some are church-goers, but some are not. But what they especially are NOT is ho-hum about being Christians.

They talk about Jesus Christ openly . . . as children talk about Santa Claus, as teenagers talk about cars or rock stars, as football fans talk about the Super Bowl. Jesus is written all over their faces . . . oozes out of their ears . . . and lights up their eyes. They're SOLD. And will try to sell anybody else who gives 'em half an opening.

They're born-again . . . they spread their Good News as if they just heard it **today** for the very first time.

They so openly proclaim Jesus Christ that, I confess, it made me uncomfortable at first. In fact, it still does. I'm nowhere near "used to it."

They are **fanatics** about Jesus.

And I am not.
Why am I not?
Are you?
Why are you not?
Is the church?
Why is it not?

Jesus was certainly a **fanatic** about God. And so were Stephen and Peter and Paul . . . and so **many** men and women of the early church . . . to the point of martyrdom.

Then why are we content to monotonously "maintain" the church, with so little passion and even less progress?

And so - having lunch alone one day in a restaurant - I began to wonder what God thinks of us (His church). I wondered what He would **say** to us about it.

Suddenly, from somewhere - the words came into my head: "LET ME OUT! . . . I'm a prisoner in a stained-glass jail!" I wrote it on my paper napkin. And as quickly as I could scribble, I filled twelve more napkins . . . then several dozen more. It felt like I was taking dictation.

However, that phenomenon happens to authors on occasion, so . . .

This book is my **fictional** version of what God MIGHT say to us. Please - if you're perplexed because I seem to have "put words in God's mouth" - please be assured that these thoughts are presented only as what **I THINK** He MIGHT say.

Some of it, of course, He did say: You will recognize a lot of biblical foundation. But since it is not my purpose to "prove" or substantiate anything (my only aims are to share and perhaps to **stir** some zeal) I have made no attempt to quote or footnote scriptural passages.

Some of it came from Christians-I-have-met: devoted disciples surely and prophets perhaps. Particularly those men and women whose evangelism goes far beyond verbal witness. They astound me. Their Christ-like selflessness, charity, sacrifice, and risk in **action** are the antithesis of a "comfortable Christianity" or hedonism that so many of us have settled for.

And some of this book came just from my own feelings and my **yearnings** for the church to be more effective - to become in behalf of God and mankind, everything He expects and knows we **can** be.

I wrote this book - with love, I hope - for all those who do love or could love the church. The book, I hope, is inspirational because SOMEHOW we **must** get inspired.

The church's mission has passively wallowed too long. And the church . . . in my opinion . . . is the only genuine hope for the world.

Wally Armbruster